SEVEN FOR LUCK

(A Song Cycle for Soprano and Orchestra)

Vocal with Piano Reduction

Music by JOHN WILLIAMS
Text by RITA DOVE

ISBN 0-634-00575-8

For all works contained herein:
Unauthorized copying, arranging, adapting, recording or public performance
is an infringement of copyright. Infringers are liable under the law.

Visit Hal Leonard Online at
www.halleonard.com

7777 W. BLUEMOUND RD. P.O. BOX 138 9 MILWAUKEE, WI 53213

Rita Dove, the Pulitzer Prize-winning author and poet and former Poet Laureate of the United States, is certainly one of our country's most distinguished literary figures. Her group of poems, which she entitled "Seven For Luck," presented wonderful material for songs, and I treasure my collaboration with this outstanding woman. In these poems, Ms. Dove writes with wit and wisdom of the many phases of a woman's life, including adolescence, courting, love, pregnancy, betrayal, and renewal.

I'm particularly pleased to add this version for voice and piano to the original, which was written for soprano and orchestra. The premiere, which I conducted with the Boston Symphony Orchestra at Tanglewood in 1998, featured the solo part brilliantly performed by Cynthia Hayman.

John Williams

SEVEN FOR LUCK

(A Song Cycle for Soprano and Orchestra)

Text by RITA DOVE

Music by JOHN WILLIAMS

1. Song

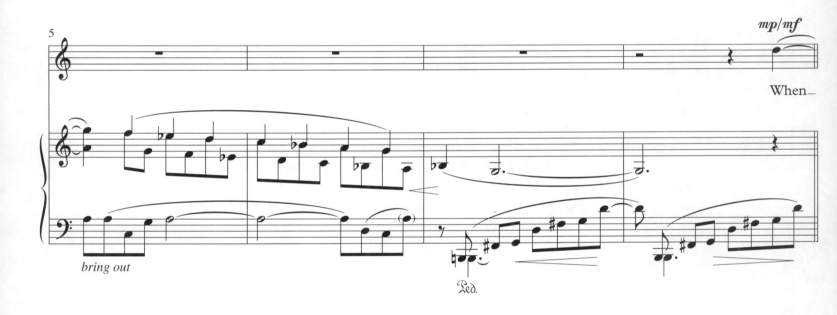

Music Copyright © 1997 by Marjer Music Corp.
Text Copyright © 1997 by Rita Dove
All Rights Reserved   Used by Permission

moon spoke in rid-dles_____ and the stars rhymed._____

I was a new toy

wait-ing_____ wait - ing___ for___ my___

own-er to pick me up.___

When

I was young,

I ran the day to it's

knees. There were trees to swing on, crick-ets to cap-ture.

"dry and light"

I was nar - row-ly sweet, in - fi-nite-ly cruel, tongued_ in

hon - ey and cod - dled_ in milk,

sun - burned and

sil-ver-y and scabbed_ like_ a colt.

And the world was al-read-y old. And I was old-er than I am to-day.

2. Chocolate

I — hold up to sniff be-tween fin - ger and thumb how you numb me with your rich at - ten - tions!

If I don't eat you

dark punch of earth and night and leaf, for a taste____ of

you.____

An - y

wom - an would glad - ly crum - ble to____

3. Adolescence

grass - es and whis-pered:_____

Lin-da's face hung be-fore us,_____ pale as a pe - can,_____ and it grew

wise as she said: "A boy's lips_____ are soft,_____ as

soft_____ as ba - by's skin."_____

4. Black on a Saturday Night

col - or   cal - cu - lat - ed   to flash   lem - on,   bronze,___ ce - rise,

in   the course   of   a   dip and a   turn._____

Beau   -   ty's   been   caught_____   ly   -   ing

and the truth's been rubbed raw: Here

you get your re - morse as a con - sti - tu - t'nal right.

It's al - ways what we don't fear that

hap - pens, al - ways not now and why are you peo - ple act - ing this way?

might as well— keep danc - - - ing keep— danc -

ing 'til to - mor - row gives up with a shout, 'cause there

is on - ly Sat - ur - day night, and we're in it

almost Spoken:

black as black can,

5. Serenade

heart-break lives on_____ when mem-o-ry's died._____

Look_ for me_____ be-hind your eyes_____ lis-ten to me_____

___ when some-one sighs.

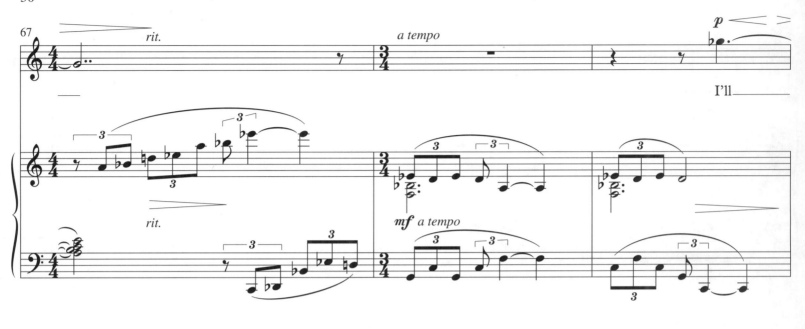

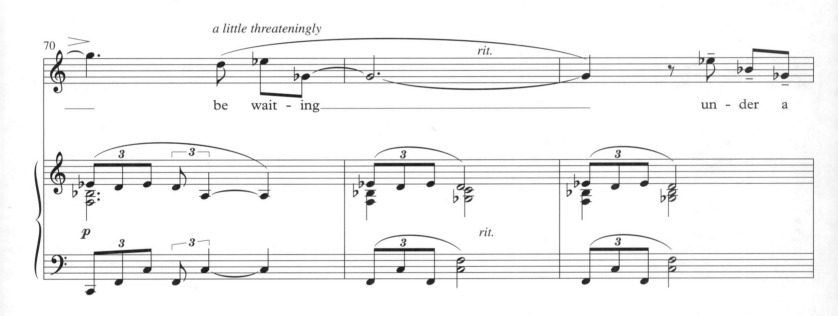

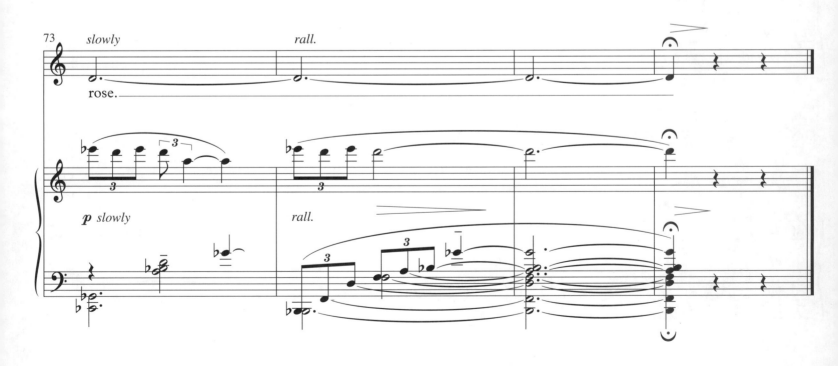

6. Expecting

Ev - 'ry wish will find its sym - bol,

the wom-an thinks.

The con-spir-a-cy's to make us thin.

Size threes are all of the rage, and skirts bal-loon-ing, ba-

loon-ing, ba-loon-ing a - bove twinkl - ing knees. Are ev - 'ry

man - childs pre-ad-o-les-cent dream. Ta-bu-la Ro-sa.

Spoken:
boldly

No slate's that clean!

We've earned our na - vels sunk in grief. Our mus - cles

say, we've been used yes, used! Have you ev-er tried

silk sheets? I did. Per - suad - ed by

post - na - tal dread and a

7. Starting Over

Just when hope with-ers— a re - prieve is grant-ed— and a

door o - pens— a re - prieve— is— grant-ed.

The win-dows you've closed be-hind you—

— are turn-ing pink— do - ing what they— do ev - 'ry dawn—

poco mouvt.

you did,   as— you   did,   when your

moth - er told— you——— what it took   to be a

wom-an———————— in   this   life.———